# HAUNTED UNIVERSE

●

# HAUNTED UNIVERSE

## The True Knowledge of Enlightenment

•

Steven Norquist

revised edition

# HAUNTED UNIVERSE
## The True Knowledge of Enlightenment
### revised edition

*Front and back cover images: visible light image of the Helix Nebula*
*The Helix Nebula, also known as The Helix or NGC 7293, is a large planetary nebula located in the constellation of Aquarius. Discovered by Karl Ludwig Harding, probably before 1824, this object is one of the closest to the Earth of all the bright planetary nebulae.*
*The estimated distance is about 215 parsecs or 700 light-years. The Helix has often been referred to as the 'Eye of God' on the internet, since about 2003.*

Credit: NASA, ESA, and C. R. O'Dell (Vanderbilt University)

Excerpt from 'Professor Nobody's Little Lectures on Supernatural Horror' by Thomas Ligotti printed with permission from the author.

Printed in the United States of America

ISBN: 1-4528-5966-3

BOOK DESIGN BY JESÚS OLMO  www.jesusolmo.com

# HAUNTED UNIVERSE

·

# ACKNOWLEDGMENTS

I can never give enough thanks to Jesús Olmo for his constant support, amazing creativity and tireless efforts to present the words of *Haunted Universe* in a way that is beautiful, unique and perfectly emphasizes the power and mood of each and every phrase. If not for Jesús Olmo *Haunted Universe* would just be a text file lost somewhere on my PC.

Thank you Jesús.

I want to extend my special thanks and appreciation to Thomas Ligotti for inspiring me to create this revision of *Haunted Universe* and for his invaluable suggestions and guidance in the editing and refining process. He challenged me to present *Haunted Universe* in its most pure and powerful form and to more precisely write what I knew to be true.

Thank you Thomas.

Steven Norquist

# ·CONTENTS·

# INTRODUCTION

Back in 2002 I woke up. The experience was blinding, crushing, soul-wrenching, and completely ordinary, a non-event of the highest magnitude. My friends and family noticed a change, though no real change took place. It seems they believed I spoke differently, saw things differently than before. But ultimately nothing was different at all.

A year after this I was chatting by email with Jordan Gruber, the creator of www.enlightenment.com. After a few exchanges he wrote this: "You really should write something when you can."

At first I had no interest in writing anything – I mean, what could a person really say about this subject? But a few days later I found myself sitting in front of the computer staring at a blank word document at about 2 a.m. I started to type and about three hours later the essay *"What is enlightenment, no, I mean really, like what is it?"* emerged.

I sent this essay to Jordan and he posted it on www.enlightenment.com. The essay got a lot of traffic and eventually found links or reposts on different sites throughout the Internet. I read the responses to this essay and got quite a few emails from people about it. In 2010, seven years after the essay, and eight years distant from the awakening, I decided it was time to write again.

Why?

Maturity? Experience? Seasoning?

Perhaps.

But there were also questions asked by those who had read my original essay that needed answers.

So I was prompted – motivated, you might say – to write again.

But how much can really be said about Enlightenment?

You see, when Enlightenment is spoken about "directly" when the universe manifests as the truth—the Ultimate Truth—then the revelation of Enlightenment is by nature short and vicious.

*Haunted Universe* is a book that has the potential to guide "he" or "she"; to the place where they will have the chance to contact reality, to experience it.

Whether *Haunted Universe* can succeed is dependent on you. Are you willing to put aside your beliefs, your preconceptions, if only briefly. To be opened to a new perception, a different level of knowing?

Can you relax your mind and judgments long enough to find something precious?

Is it possible to accept that there might be something that you have not seen, something that is immediately appearing before your eyes daily, yet somehow has escaped your detection?

If you can do this, if only briefly, then *Haunted Universe* has something to say to you.

But do you really want to read this book?

Perhaps not.

There is much at stake . . . much.

Though you have the potential to change your life forever, change of this type will not come without cost.

There will be casualties.

Physical, emotional, spiritual, and social casualties.

You will be invited to contemplate a path to destruction, to existential suicide.

False beliefs will be dispelled, lies seen through.

My advice is to just forget the whole Enlightenment thing and go back to your life.

However, I know there are those who will ignore this advice and read on.

To those who do, know this:

We are about to enter dark realms, haunted realms, where spirituality and bliss are hors d'oeuvres and souls the main course.

Mist on a lake, fog in thick woods, a golden light shining on wet stones—such sights make it all very easy. Something lives in the lake, rustles through the woods, inhabits the stones or the earth beneath them. Whatever it may be, this *something* lies just out of sight, but not out of vision for the eyes that never blink. In the right surroundings our entire being is made of eyes that dilate to witness the haunting of the universe. But really, do the right surroundings have to be so obvious in their spectral atmosphere? Take a cramped waiting room, for instance. Everything there seems so well-anchored in normalcy. Others around you talk ever so quietly; the old clock on the wall is sweeping aside the seconds with its thin red finger; the window blinds deliver slices of light from the outside world and shuffle them with shadows. Yet at any time and in any place, our bunkers of banality may begin to rumble. You see, even in a stronghold of our fellow beings we may be subject to abnormal fears that would land us in an asylum if we voiced them to another. Did we just feel some presence that does not belong among us? Do our eyes see something in a corner of that room in which we wait for we know not what? Just a little doubt slipped into the mind, a little trickle of suspicion in the bloodstream, and all those eyes of ours, one by one, open up to the world and see its horror. Then: no belief or body of laws will guard you; no friend, no counselor, no appointed personage will save you; no locked door will protect you; no private office will hide you. Not even the solar brilliance of a summer day will harbor you from horror. For horror eats the light and digests it into darkness.

Thomas Ligotti
*Professor Nobody's Little Lectures on Supernatural Horror*

HAUNTED UNIVERSE

The universe you live in is haunted.

Perhaps you have noticed this.

There are things happening that cannot be explained.

Maybe you have never experienced anything like this.

Maybe you have never questioned the very reality
that appears before your eyes.

But you should.

Because something is roaming out there
in the silence, haunting this universe.

Its origin is from the beginning.

Its power: the animation of existence.

The consequences of its discovery: the end of life.

And it is not far from you.

Maybe you have felt its touch?

The icy prickle of the void.

There have always been those who
throughout time have known of this haunting.

They have sensed that just beyond the boundary
of what is understood as life there is
something dark and powerful.

Having approached the boundary
they have felt this haunting.

Eerily silent, infinitely empty.

And having perceived this haunting, if only vaguely,
they have turned away from it in horror.

Those that have turned away did so instinctively.

They sensed the danger, they felt the risk.
They knew innately that their very being was in peril.

But there are some who have not turned away, who have dared to cross that boundary, to master their fear and move forward towards the essence of what haunts this universe.

They too have felt the fear and the horror of what it might mean to move forward, but the pain, anger, depression and hopelessness of life demanded that they know if there was an answer, some final answer to the questions that plague humanity.

Who am I? Why am I here? Is there a God?

A person can only live so long in a dream
before a nightmare must emerge.

And once that nightmare emerges and dominates the field of consciousness the urge to awaken manifests.

Like a sleeping person who sits up suddenly in bed and shakes off the effects of their nightmare, so a waking person seeks release from the nightmare that they have now recognized as life.

But as the sleeping person will wake from their nightmare, and in that waking the dream world they had previously inhabited will vanish, not so for the waking person.

The waking person must be aware that the nightmare that is their daily life, or even the wonderful dream that is their daily life, will not vanish.

Instead, in real Awakening it is the "dreamer"
that vanishes.

When people finally begin to move beyond themselves,
when they are finally ready to cross that boundary and
confront the ancient darkness that haunts this universe,
it is then they will know that the dream never ends,
it is only "they" who will end.

It is not the dream that has deceived them, it is they who have deceived themselves.

As they stand in the midst of the dream, the experience of Awakening is not the dissolution of the fabric of reality around them, but instead the vanishing of themselves.

The dream glows with increasing brilliance in the same

moment as the individual becomes

dim and insubstantial.


It is at this point that many will do all in their power

to remain, to reenter the dream, to keep from fading.

They feel the cost of full Awakening, of full
Enlightenment, and it is a horrible thing.

It is not the bliss that was promised,
or the joy they hoped for.

Instead everything they knew and loved are going.

All their hopes, all their aspirations, everything that
made them uniquely them are vanishing.

They are dying.

No, it is more than dying:

They are being annihilated.

And this annihilation is final.

They have directly perceived the true nature of reality.

And its destructive power is irrevocable.

But in the midst of this destruction is experienced the surprise of Awakening: With the death of the individual it is learned that no individual has died.

There never was a dreamer.

Nothing has been lost.

And it is suddenly clear now what haunts this universe.

The universe is haunted by silence, by emptiness.

There is only activity without author,
manifestation without mind.

A dream without a dreamer.

What sages from every era have come to understand is this simple truth: All that happens in this universe does so spontaneously, perfectly, and of its own accord.

Yet simultaneously and equally true in this spontaneous manifestation that is the universe, is the knowledge that nothing is random; everything emerges exactly as it has to.

The great sages have learned this not by theory
but by direct experience.

You know this is true.

You *feel* it.

You may deny it or distract yourself from
the *feeling* of it, but if you sit quietly and really listen,
you will hear what the sages have heard:

the hum of the machine, working endlessly,
blindly and perfectly.

This is the Ultimate Truth,
the revelation that none return from.

To the one who discovers Ultimate Truth, who becomes enlightened, such a one will realize that they have changed tremendously and that everything they have ever loved or valued is gone forever.

Yet, they simultaneously know that in this happening, everything is exactly the same; not one iota of existence has moved one speck from its previous course.

The Ultimate Truth reveals that the only thing going on in the universe is spontaneous manifestation.

Perfect, automatic, machine-like emergence.

The substance of this emergence is consciousness.

The very fabric of space/time is consciousness.

Consciousness is all there is or ever could be.

Remember this equation:

$$U = C$$

( Universe = Consciousness )

They are one and the same.

Consciousness is not a perception,
a sense that allows you to be aware of something.

There is nothing like that.

Consciousness is the Universe. The Universe is
Consciousness. They are one, they are
the reality—the only reality, the Ultimate Truth.

There isn't, nor will there ever be, any "one" or "thing" that is "aware".

It has been said, "Life is but a dream."

The universe is an ongoing dream without a dreamer,
a grand play with no performers and no audience.

Enlightenment is the sound of a pebble
rolling down a hill on a planet in a star system
that you will never know.

This is how it *feels*.

THE PRICE

Do you want to die?

Be burned to ash?

Have your life ripped from you?

Do you want the clear and irrevocable understanding in the heart of your being that everything, every single thing up to this very moment of your life has been complete lies and bullshit?

Do you want that?

To cry and mourn all that is?

To finally stand alone and unconnected to any human
purpose or endeavor forever?

Does this sound even close to what
you are looking for?

Because if you are foolish enough to proceed
forward then the only reward for your struggle
will be total annihilation.

"You" will be lost forever.

"You" will never return.

There is no happiness at the end of that tunnel,
the light is not waiting for you.

There is only the crushing silence of the abyss.

People think the Ultimate Truth will make their life better, that they will finally know love or peace.

It is not like this.

But make no mistake, having the Ultimate Truth is the most important thing that could ever be. Once obtained you would never trade what you will learn and then experience on a daily basis for any treasure or pleasure in this life or the next.

All life compared to the Ultimate Truth is filth,
dust that can be swept into the void.

And make no mistake, life, "your life," will be swept into the void to obtain the Ultimate Truth. This is the trade that must take place, the terms of the deal you will make with the Devil.

Love, Joy, Happiness?

Filth by comparison to living fully in the Ultimate Truth.

Do you want to one day know
what is really going on?

Then approach the Ultimate Truth
with horror and hatred.

That is the only way you can proceed.

You are walking the short walk to the gallows,
there is no more time for lies.

When you feel the fire of the rope, oblivion is only a
short drop away. Do you want the moment between
those two instants to be filled with lies?

Right now the rope is tightly around your neck, the executioner has his hand on the lever and the time from now until he pulls it is the rest of your life.

How will you spend it?

In lies, bullshit, and delusion?

Or will you scream forth into the void in horror and hatred demanding a glimpse, if only for a second, of the Ultimate Truth, before your spine is torn from your body?

It all comes down to this:

When you have crossed over and entered into final awakening you will look back and laugh. This is simply how it will be. Everything will be self apparent, natural once you have awakened.

The barrier to Ultimate Truth that you currently face
is your own desire for meaning or value.

There is no meaning or value, there never has been.

The sooner you can understand this, the sooner
you can find the pristine clarity that has never not been.

And when you finally begin to break through
that barrier you may experience suffering, anger,
hopelessness or depression as everything
you once held dear begins to be lost.

These feelings are the death rattles,

the crunching of metal and roaring of the

steam furnaces as the icy ocean pours into the hull

of a great ship and pulls it down into the depths.


The mighty vessel fights this to the last

and then it is under.


And as the final ripples settle,

only stillness remains.


The moon shines down on the surface of the ocean

and the view is perceived as one of utter beauty,

utter perfection.

*Feel* this emptiness, this clarity, this crystalline transparency that is the universe.

You are that which moves - mindless, intentionless.

Never dying, yet never born.

Do you *feel* it?

You are awakening, it is happening.

You reach down for your child's hand and
there is no one there.

You turn to your lover and see only a pillow that has not been slept upon.

You look in the mirror and see only the wall behind you.

You are gone, finally and irrevocably.

You see the universe now, at last, as it is.

And you smile.

GOOD, EVIL AND PERFECTION

There is no good.

There is no evil.

There are no acts.

The universe is perfect.

When you awaken you will see this,
you will feel/know it.

No questions of morality will remain.

You will directly feel/know that all emerges mindless,
thoughtless and spontaneously without even
the slightest randomness.

*"War is hell"* they say. *"We have to bring peace,*
*we have to work for a better world."*

There is no better world.

The very thought that a world could be changed for the better is the darkest evil, the darkest delusion.

Every person that ever raised a flag was completely insane.

Yet they did nothing wrong.

There is no act in this universe
that could ever be wrong.

Why?

Because there are no acts.

The universe is filled with happenings with no author,
actions with no actor.

Things that seem to be personal are not.

No one exists or has performed anything, ever.

Silence is moving in emptiness,
acting actionless in the void.

You do not exist.

You have never existed.

You will never exist.

You are not reading this.

A puppet is dangling.

The universe is moving.

Millions are dying.

All are safe.

Do you understand?

The towers came down and the victims were grateful.


Grateful...

Mother Teresa fed a starving child.

A pedophile raped a boy.

A star went super nova ten thousand years ago

and a trillion beings were vaporized.

A seal is laughing as it frolics.

A Great White shark tears it to shreds.

The blood in the water fades quickly into nothingness.

All is as it is.

*"We believe God has a plan. Things may seem bad now but it is all working out for the greater good."*

Prevarication.

*"There must be a purpose to existence,*
*a reason why I am here?"*

Delusion.

*"Life has no meaning, I want to kill myself
to end the pain."*

Blindness.

There is nothing wrong, nothing to fix.

No flag needs to be raised.

No war needs to be fought.

Justice is blind.

There is neither good nor evil.

The universe manifests, and just that is perfection.

TRUTH AND SUFFERING

The Ultimate Truth is the most natural thing that could ever be. It is the reality, the very nature of all that is.

And the ease with which the Ultimate Truth manifests is laughable.

People have struggled for so long to find it, to grasp it.

But they are fools.

They have approached the Ultimate Truth
with vulgarity.

They have impugned its perfection with their
insatiable gluttony.

They have asked that the Ultimate Truth remove
their suffering.

They have asked that the Ultimate Truth will make them
happy, that it will give them joy and endless bliss.

Blasphemy.

The Ultimate Truth is the fires of hell.

A flaming column of destruction.

A whirlwind of annihilation.

Anyone who would approach it must do so with the full knowledge that they will be seared from existence.

The Ultimate Truth will suffer no illusions.

Anyone who comes to it with hope must be torn apart.

It has been said that they who find
the Ultimate Truth will cease to suffer, that suffering
itself is an illusion rooted firmly in the false belief that
what manifests before your eyes is actually real.

It has been said that if you can only realize that
all you see is an illusion, you can finally be free
and finally know an end to suffering.


Lies.

Suffering never ends.

Worlds die.

Galaxies fall into oblivion.

Civilizations become extinct.

The rape of Nanking goes on forever.

There will never be an end to suffering, never, as long as the greatest deception ever spun continues to be loved, nursed and protected.

The primary error – the assumption of being,
the assumption of self.

This is the curse on humanity.

The fall of man.

The beginning of sorrows.

Manifestation is not an illusion.

The only illusion is the belief that
there could be something or someone.

That being exists.

No.

There is no being, there is no self.

There are no beings in existence in this universe.

But not only that, there is no higher self,
no ultimate being.

A look behind the curtain proves, there is no one there.

There never has been.

There is only Universe/Consciousness
manifesting spontaneously and perfectly.

Do you want your suffering to end?

Then lose the hope for affirmation of being
and you will find the peace and release of the void.

Emptiness is the natural state of reality,
it can only be felt/known.

You must feel/know it. Once you feel/know it
then you will finally be free.

Don't let anyone deceive you - *you* must disappear.

Affirmation of being is the work of Satan;
only in annihilation can there be final rest.

And once you are destroyed?

Then the suffering that comes from the belief that you must have meaning or purpose to live will be gone.

Finally the constant pain that forces you to seek after something, that makes you quest to find something, some purpose, will be ended.

Love, success, hope, recognition.

Everything that was grasped at before the Ultimate Truth will be seen after the Ultimate Truth for the sheer bullshit that it has always been.

It is horrible and hilarious.

Once all that vacuousness is seen for what it truly is,

then all the suffering contingent upon

it is also extinguished.

And once that suffering ends,
it is impossible to pick it up again.

But here is the paradox:

In that revelation and knowing is the
final destruction of the individual.

No one will remain to feel the freedom from delusion,
the freedom from suffering.

There is only the haunting silence of the universe that has always only been.

THE DRAGON

People want to meditate and gain Enlightenment.

If they knew for one second what that really means
they would spring back in terror.

The spiritual path today is concerned with the improvement of man and an understanding of his place in the universe.

There is nothing like this.

There is no one to improve, no good deeds to be done, no world peace to be gained.

The best a fully Awakened person can hope for is the slow dissolution of their being, as the shadow of their ego fades into the oblivion it emerged from.

In the heart of each and every person lives a singularity – a black hole, an irresistible void – and no so-called person or ego will ever know peace until they fade away back into the abyss that birthed them.

This void is the origin of all things.

It is not love, or care, or hate, or peace; it is ultimate goneness, ultimate loss, ultimate freedom.

Death is the greatest gift that was ever
given to humanity.

Why do you think life does everything
in its power to return to death?

Everything from particle to galaxy falls
into death and is glad.

People fear death for many reasons. They love their family and don't want to lose them, they have a life and want to keep enjoying it, they have things to do, and so on.

All lies.

The one who seeks freedom, true radical freedom, must walk this earth as the living dead.

All their life and vitality must be sapped away, all their hopes and dreams must be swallowed into darkness.

Only as a zombie, a vampire, a ghost can the
Awakened walk if they choose to.

Yet the Awakened choose sleep and darkness as the
closest they can come on this earth to final release
into reality.

Deep down you know this is true,
yet these thoughts horrify you.

Horror is a correct feeling.

Think for a moment about horror.

Not the horror of rapists or mass-murderers or other self-involved persons.

*Pure* horror.

Something monstrous beyond anything in this world.

A dragon.

The Dragon of Enlightenment.

What characteristics of the Ultimate Truth are
epitomized in The Dragon of the Enlightenment?

Sleep, darkness.

The Dragon sleeps the blissful sleep of full Awakening.

The Dragon has seen the Ultimate Truth, and in that
Ultimate Truth the Dragon seeks the peace
of darkness and slumber.

The Dragon never goes out to harm, instead it is always some external disturbance that forces it to destroy—to become a horror.

The Dragon sleeps deep in its cave until some fool disturbs it.

The Dragon awakes from its blissful slumber, stretches out its wings and expresses the other characteristic of Ultimate Truth, the flames of annihilation.

Only when the fool who woke him – and the village –
are scorched from the earth does the Dragon return to
its cave to resume the blissful sleep of full Awakening.

Do not wake the Dragon or you will be consumed.

The hurricane shatters the coast and then rests.

The volcano destroys the village, and then rests.

The earthquake buries the city and then rests.

The Ultimate Truth is rest, stillness, sleep.

The instant that human ego tries to assert itself:
suffering, flames, destruction,
annihilation, peace – in that order.

It has been said:

"The universe is perfect; intervene at your peril."


Once you become awakened you will understand this.


You will feel/know it.

You will become the Dragon.

You will seek your cave and you will rest until your life
fades into the oblivion that it emerged from.

You will feel in yourself the inability to buy in,
the inability to see meaning in anything.

You will become very bored with the world.
Most, if not all, of what you enjoy will be gone.

Bit by bit you will start to lose yourself. You may fear this at first, but eventually you will have no control or care as the void sucks you down.

You will begin to feel less;

love and hate will equally slip away.


Gradually, sleep will begin to call to you.


Then one day you will find a cave and lie down.

You will resent anything that dares

to interrupt that rest, and you will become like

The Dragon of Enlightenment:


a flaming force, searing meaning and ego and hope.

ANNIHILATION

How is it that an enlightened person is able to seem to live a life, to give good advice, to care, to help, and generally to have fun?

These enlightened ones have perfected
the art of automation.

They have ceased to exist not only in reality,
which was always the case,
but also in their own minds.

They are like animatronics characters from Disneyland.

They are simply a shell following its programming.

Again, the universe is in charge.

They are not acting – there are no deliberate acts –

there is only the universe spontaneously and perfectly

manifesting as and through them.

The enlightened know this is the way it is. The enlightened know there is no need to try to change or be something other than what they have always been, right up to the moment of Enlightenment.

Once annihilation takes place – once the ego, the personality, all hope and all dreams are gone (and make no mistake, all of that is an instantaneous process in the moment of realization, though its effect may play out over time) – then within that split second of realization is also the absolutely profound shock that nothing at all has changed.

Enlightenment will sear out your eyes, melt the flesh from your bones, tear out your heart, sacrifice it to the sun and leave you completely, irrevocably, unchanged.

Radical change produces sameness.

Paradox and perfection.

You have always been a mindless, soulless, animatronics character in Disneyland with music and dancing and singing and flashing lights and absolutely no one ever in the park to see or experience it.

So why would an enlightened person ever do anything different than before Enlightenment?

They don't; they never have.

You see, there has only ever been Enlightenment,

actionless, motionless, and as active

as a two-year-old child.


In the end, act or don't act – they are both the same.


In the end, nothing is happening or ever could.

Once you are enlightened, you will observe a solemn moment of silence for the death of a good friend, smile, and then go back to what you were doing and live out your life with gusto or disdain.

The Ultimate Truth is a sledgehammer to the nose,
and anyone who doesn't know they have been hit
with it is either dead, comatose, or high.
And when it hits, that's it.

Story over.

You get up, pay your tab, put on your hat,
and leave the bar.

You're done.

And when that first gust of night air hits, you laugh, or smile, or just nod to yourself, put your head down, pull your collar up and vanish into the darkness…

REBIRTH

You are invisible, insubstantial, truly formless.

You have no boundaries;
you can neither be contained nor defined.

Where are you?

Are you at all?

These questions no longer arise for you.

You see and feel with each day only emptiness,
only stillness, only clarity.

It is as if all of time is standing still for you.

As if all you observe is motionless, frozen.

When you move you are like light moving through a universe made of flawlessly transparent crystal.

The ease with which you now move is beyond joy, or bliss.

You realize now that any blessing that was ever conceived of as being conferred through gaining Enlightenment was delusion.

No human mind could ever have conceived

what the Ultimate Truth would really be like.

And you now exist fully as this Ultimate Truth

for all eternity.


But you know immediately it has always been this way.

Stretching back into untold eons and forward to unknown infinity this ease and silence and rest has always been all there ever was.

You know you do not exist, not in the sense the world understands existence, and you are very glad.

You are no longer constrained;
you expand outwards and fill all that is.

And in that expansion and filling you understand,

you have never been constrained;

you have never not filled all that is.


You laugh at the absurdity of it,

that anyone would not know this.


It is right there!


How can they not see it?

Yet you know they do see it, this is the paradox:
They see it and live it each day and yet they are dying
alone in the pain of never finding it.

But you do not mourn them, this too is as it is.

There is no sadness in you, or in them.

Wonderful paradox, beautiful beyond
words or thoughts.

You see now that this is the very nature
and beauty of infinite ease.

There is nothing to be done anymore,
no one to help, no task to accomplish.

There is not the slightest movement away from this
perfection that could ever accomplish
anything of value.

This is understood fully now, seen clearly at last.

There are no more doubts.

The power of this realization is horrible in its beauty, stunning in its destruction, overwhelming in a way that can never be expressed.

You shrink in cowardice and move forward boldly in the same act.

You are like a baby looking at its mother's face
for the first time, there is awe and worship.

But when the breast is offered you lose yourself in her.

You also understand there is a world out there,
a dream.

Like the Dragon of Enlightenment you now sleep with one eye open.

The horror is done, the smoke has cleared and the embers are finally cold.

A choice is now before you.

Something can emerge from those ashes.

But what might emerge will never be the same as what was once believed to be.

How will you navigate the dream?

Who will you be?

Will you take on the old role, now refined and alive, which is perfectly acceptable, or will you create a new costume to wear?

You need not decide now, time is your friend.

Your awakening was sudden,
your annihilation terrible in its ferocity.

You immediately saw all there ever was to see.

But you understand now that a process is unfolding,

a play is being enacted.


This process has always been what is,

but now you see it unfolding.

Waves are rolling in and you are no longer drowning.

You sit young and strong on your surf board,
legs dangling in the warm ocean.

The tropical sun heats your naked skin.

The waves keep coming.

But you are in no hurry now.

You will wait for the one worth the ride.

And when it comes, you will stand up with awe and worship, and then lose yourself in it.

# Haunted Press

www.HauntedPress.net

19607862R00106

Made in the USA
Lexington, KY
28 December 2012